AF535097
FROM THE LIBRARY OF

BEAR RIGHT

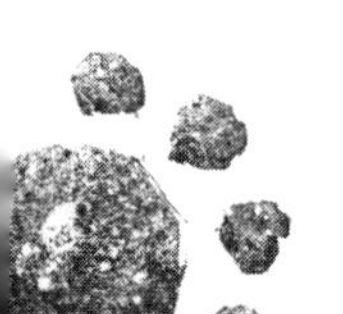

AN UNEXBEARGATED
COMPBEARHENSIVE
INCOMPBEARABLE
BOOK OF

CELEBEARTIES & OTHER BEARS

BY PHYLLIS DEMONG

PAUL S. ERIKSSON
Publisher
MIDDLEBURY, VERMONT

Printed in the United States of America.
987654321

Library of Congress Cataloging in Publication Data

Demong, Phyllis.
Celebearties & other bears.

1. Biography—20th century—Caricatures and cartoons. 2. American wit and humor, Pictorial. 3. Puns and punning. I. Title.
NC1429.D363A4 1979 741.5'973 79-13533
ISBN 0-8397-1332-0

FOR
DEE
HEYWOOD

INTRODUCTION

FROM BEARKLEY CALIFORNIA TO THE BEARRING SEA, FROM BEARNE SWITZERLAND TO NORTHERN SIBEARIA, THE WORLD HAS LONG YEARNED AND BEARNED FOR A COMPBEARHENSIVE INCOMPBEARABLE UNEXBEARGATED BOOK OF BEARS

AND HERE IT IS . . .

THIS BOOK HAS BEEN BRUIN FOR QUITE A-WHILE, AND THOUGH FILLED WITH PUNS BOTH BEARABLE AND UNBEARABLE, IT REPBEARSENTS ONLY THE TIP OF THE ICEBEARG.

ACKNOWLEDGEMENT IS DUE TO THOSE WHO HELPED BEAR THE BEARDEN OF SCHOLARLY RESEARCH • TO TIM ATKINS OF THE BEAR NECESSITIES (THE BEARON OF THE BEAR INDUSTRY • WITH SHOPS COAST-TO-COAST) TO HIS ASSISTANT BARBEARA—TO JEAN BEARADSHAW LYTTLE—AND TO MY DOG BEARANDY WHOSE BEAR-LIKE NOSE HAS BEEN A CONSTANT INSBEARATION • BEARCI • (THAT'S FRENCH FOR THANK YOU). THE AUTHOR

MIDDLEBEARY, BEARMONT

CELEBEARTIES

RICHARD BEARTON

SARAH BEARNHART

LIBEARACE
(holding candleabeara)

VICTOR HERBEART
(writing an opbearetta)

JOHN BEARRYMORE
(as Shakesbeare's Hamlet)

HERBEART HOOBEAR

ABEARHAM LINCOLN

SCHUBEART

LEONARD BEARNSTEIN
(conducting Bearlioz)

THEDA BEARA

HANK GREENBEARG

YOGI BEARRA

BEARNARD BEARUCH

FATHER BEARIGAN

BEAR BRYANT

MAX BEAR

BRIDGET BEARDOT

ALBEART EINSTEIN

BEARYSHNIKOV

SAINTE BEARNADETTE

ELIZABETH BEARETT BROWNING

JAMES BEARD

B'EAR RABBIT

BEART LAHR

(AS THE COWARDLY LION)

THE BEAR THAT MADE MILWAUKEE FAMOUS

BEART PARKS

BEARON ROTHCHILD

BEARING BEARGUNDY WINE

GEORGE BEARNARD SHAW

MORE CELEBEARTIES

ANNA BEARIA ALBEARGHETTI
CANDY BEARGEN
INGLEBEAR HUMPBEARDINK
BEARGESS MEREDITH
ALBEART CAMUS
BEARBARA STANWYCK
ALLAN GINSBEARG
HUBEART HUMBEARY
LOUIS KRONENBEARGER
BEN BEARNIE
STRINDBEARG
P. T. BEARNUM
ALGERNON SWINBEARNE
JAMES THURBEAR
CYRANO DE BEARGERAC
AMBROSE BEARCE
THORNTON BEARGESS
RICHARD CHAMBEARLIN
RUBE GOLDBEARG
JOHN BEARCH (SOCIETY)
GRIZZLY ADAMS
BEARPEE (SEEDS)
GENERAL BEARGOYNE
AARON BEARR
VINCE LOMBEARDI
WALLACE BEARY
AUBREY BEARDSLEY
CHE GUEBEARRA
DIANE VON FURSTENBEARG
FREDDIE BEARTHOLOMEW
EPHRIAM ZIMBEARLIST

CAROL BEARNETT
DAVID BEARINKLEY
BEARY MANILOW
KATHERINE HEPBEARN
GINA LOLLABEARIDGIDA
DR. CHRISTIAN BEARNARD
BLUEBEARD
ROBEART REDFORD
BEARTOLUCCI
BEART LANCE
CLAUDETTE COLBEAR
INGRID BEARGMAN
INGMAR BEARGMANN
BEARY GOLDWATER
ELY CULBEARTSON
BEARTHOLD BRECHT
ANN MORROW LINDBEARGH
RALPH WALDO EMBEARSON
ROBEART E. LEE
WILBEAR WRIGHT
BARBEARA STREISAND
GUSTAVE FLAUBEART
ROBEART FROST
CARL SANDBEARG
BARBEARA WALTERS
BEAR ABBIE
JOHN BEARSFORD TIPTON
KING HUMBEARTO
FABEARGE
SHELLEY BEARMAN
BEARLITZ

& MORE!

ELLEN BEARSTYN
BEARIO ANDRETTI
WOODWARD & BEARNSTEIN
SIR JAMES BEARRIE
BELA BEARTOK
SIR MAX BEARBOHM
BEARENDAN BEHAN
HUCKLEBEARY FINN
MARISA BEARENSEN
MILTON BEARLE
IRVING BEARLIN
HEYWOOD BRUIN
JOHN BEARLYCORN
BEARTHSHEBA
SAMUEL BEARBER

BEAR LINES

FAMILY, OCCUPATIONS & ACTIVITIES

BEARTH ANNOUNCEMENT
A NEW CUB!
Bearyl Beargina

FORE

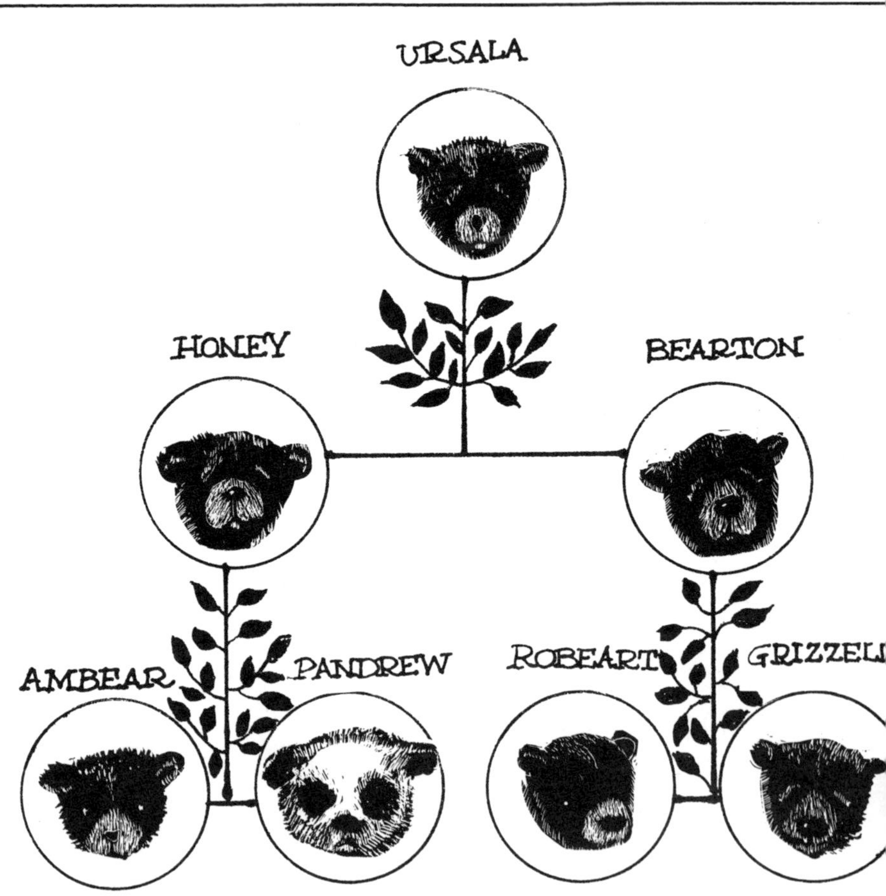

BEARS

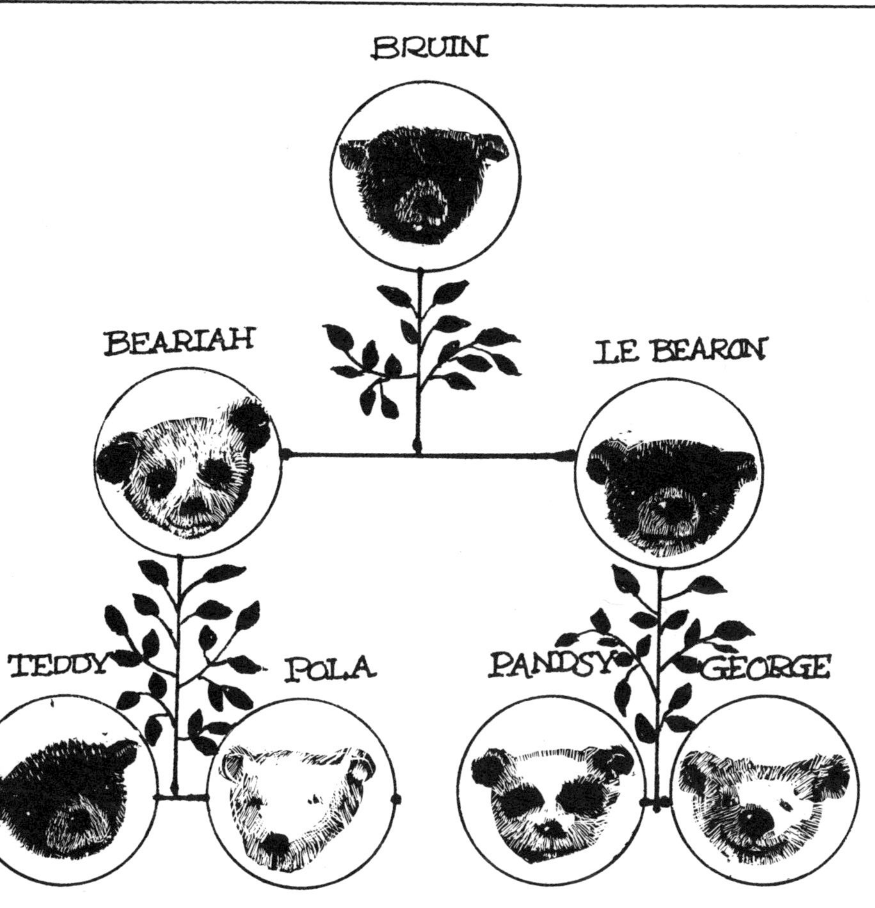

AUNT BEARTHA
WITH BEARNIECE

THE BEARRIES

LINGONBEARY · TEABEARY
STRAWBEARY · BLUEBEARY
HUCKLEBEARY · GOOSEBEARY
RAZZBEARY · BOYSENBEARY

& THE ELDERBEARRY

BEAR CHESTE

EMBEARASSED

LUMBEARJACK

WITH BEARCH TREE

TIM BEAR

BEAR HUG

BEARRELING DOWNHILL

(BEARALELL SKIER)

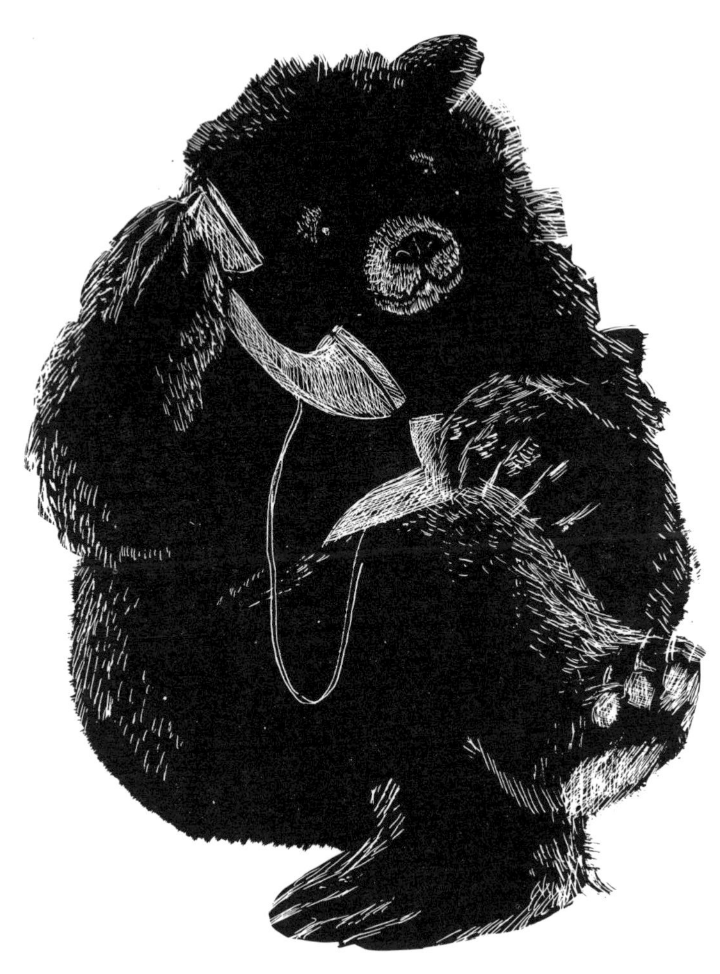

OPBEARATOR..........

WOMEN'S LIBBEAR

BEARNING HER BEARSIERRE

BEARING GIFTS BEARING ARMS

.........BEARING CHILDREN

SOMBEARO

HABEARDASHER

BEARET

APBEARATIF

SOBEAR

NOT SO SOBEAR

"BEARP"

BARBEARSHOP QUARTET

UMBEARELLA

BEARRISTER

WALL STREET BEAROKERS

WITH BEARIEF CASES

BEARSITIS

BEARICOSE VEINS

bear aspbearin

AND

BEARTENDER
INEBEARATED
BEARSERK
BEAROMETER
BEARRICADE
BEARBACK RIDER
BEARI-BEARI
SCARLET FEBEAR
AMBEARGRIS

NEIGHBEARS
BEAR-ENTHESES
ROBBEARS
SLOBBEARS
TROOPBEARS
(SMOKIES)
BEAREAVED
BEAR SKIN RUG

AND

SOME LEFTOBEARS FOR BEARUNCH

BEARMUDA ONIONS
HAMBEARGERS
BEARNAISE SAUCE
ASBEARAGAS
ICEBEARG LETTUCE
CUCUMBEARS
BEARGAMOT TEA
HUBBEARD SQUASH
CAMEMBEART
BEARRIES
BEARLEY SOUP

BEAROWNIES
RHUBEARB
POPOBEARS
CORN BEARED
BEAR-B-QUE
BEARANDY
ALEXANDER
PUMPBEARNIKEL
LOX AND BEARGEL
BEARST OF CHICKEN
BEARETZELS

ASSOCIATES

PAN

DAMONIUM!

PANDALOONS

SUSPANDARS

EXPAN

DABLE

NURSA
(with hypbeardermi

URSA MAJOR
URSA MINOR

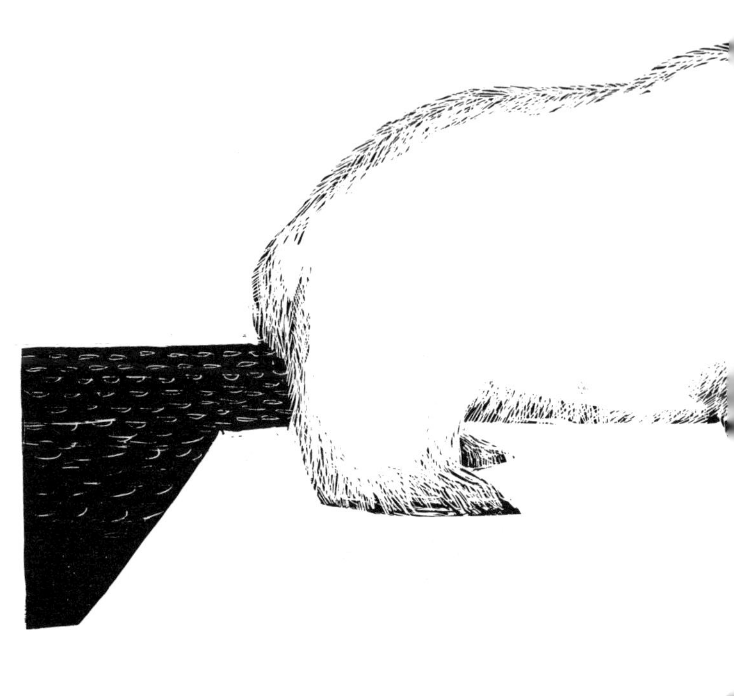

POLA

EAR ON ICEBEARG

POLARIS

POLAROIDS

POLA

RIZED

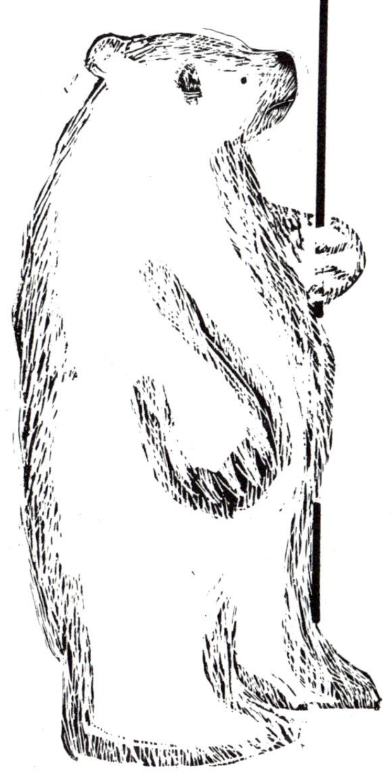

COCA KOALA
PEPSI KOALA

EKOALATY

NIGHT KOALA

KOALING ON HANDS & KNEES

OBSCENE PHONE KOALA

TEDDY ROOSEVELT

A TEDDY

AND

PANDAMERICA
PANDAORA'S BOX
PANDAHELLENIC
URSATZ
PURSANALITY
STEDDY
UNSTEDDY
TEDDY PHONE
TEDDY GRAPH
TEDDY VISION
NUMBEARS (POLAR BEARS)

RELATED SUBJECTS

tars and stripes
FOR -EBEAR

BEARITONE
(singing'If ebear I would leave you

BEAR BEARREL POLKA

CIRI·BEARI·BIN

O beary me not on the lone prairie

bears eat oats
'n does eat oats 'n ....

♪♪"eating goobear peas"♪♪

wh' oan cha be ma teddy bear

And..... a partridge
in a bear tree.

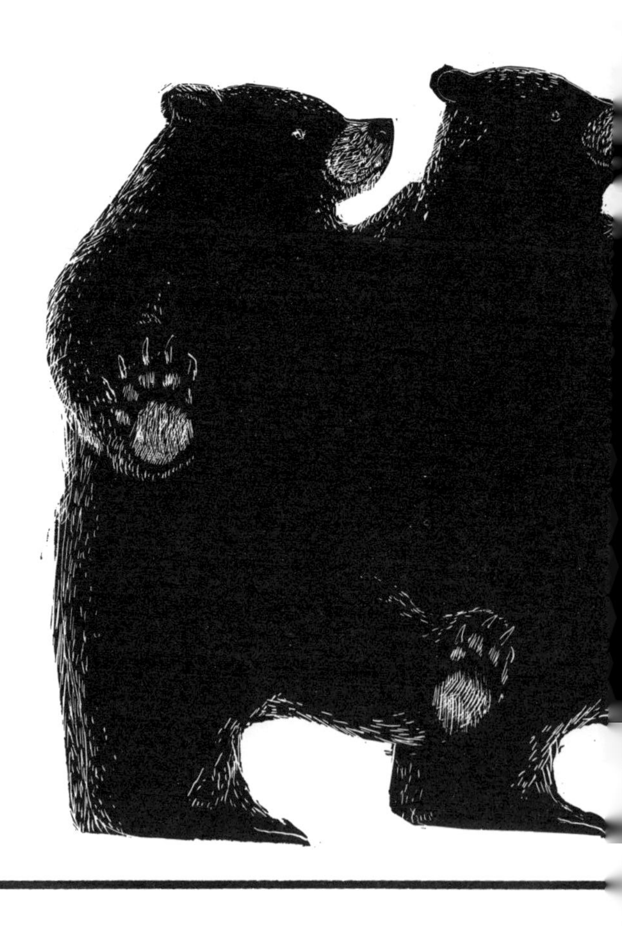

follies beargère

BEAROQUE MUSIC
ABEARICA THE BEAUTIFUL
THE NIGHTINGALE SANG IN
BEARKLEY SQUARE
BEAR WENT OVER THE MOUNTAIN
I FOUND MY LOVE ON BLUE-
BEARRY HILL
THE YELLOW SUBEARINE

BEAR
THESE DATES IN MIND

HAPPY BEARTHDAYS

BEAR MITZVAHS

ANNIBEARSARIES

SEPTEMBEAR

LABEAR DAY

BACK TO BEAROWN UNIBEARSIT

OCTOBEAR

NOVEMBEAR

DECEMBEAR

GETTING YOUR BEARR

BEARRE BEARMONT
BEARLINGTON BEARMONT
GREAT BEARRINGTON MASS.
BEARMINGHAM ALABEARMA
BEAR MT. N.Y.
BEARGEN NORWAY
BEARNE SWITZERLAND
PITTSBEARGH PA.
HARRIS-BEARGH PA.
WILKES BEARRE PA.
BEARKLEY CA.
BEARLIN GER.
BEARGUNDY FR.
BEARMUDA
BEARIA KY.
KOALA LAMPUR, MALA.
N. BRUINSWICK CANADA
S. BEARWICK ME.
BEARMA
BEARBANK CA.
IBEARIA
SIBEARIA USSR
GIBEARALTER
ALBEARTA CANADA

INGS STRAIT

LIBEARIA AFRICA
JOHANNESBEARG S.A.
BEARCELONA SPAIN
BEARU S.A.
BEARMA
EDINBEARGH SCOT.
ABEARDEEN SCOT.
BEARUT

OLD SAYINGS PROBEARBS

BEAR AND FOREBEAR
IS GOOD PHILOSOPHY

KOALA ME ANYTHING
BUT DON'T KOALA ME
LATE FOR DINNER

LIBEARTY EKOALATY
AND FRATERNITY

REMEMBEAR THE MAINE

BEAR WITH ME

GRIN AND BEAR IT

A LABEAR OF LOVE

GOD BLESS ABEARICA

BEARIN GO BRAGH

MOTTOS QUOTES CLICHÉS

BEARKING UP THE WRONG TREE

THE KOALATY OF MERCY IS NOT STRAINED . . . .

"ICH BIN EIN BEARLINER"

IN VINO BEARITAS

BEAR FOOT BOY WITH CHEEK OF TAN . . . .

PUT ON YOUR BEARAKES

BEAR RIGHT—BEAR LEFT

ARRIVABEARCI ROMA

TO SELL A BEAR ! TO SELL WHAT ONE HAS NOT

TO FIDDLE WHILE ROME BEARNS

FROM BEARAKE OF DAY 'TIL SETTING SUN
A WOMAN'S WORK IS NEBEAR DONE

BEAR PAGE

"LOVE BEARS ALL THINGS, BELIEVES ALL THINGS, ENDURES ALL THINGS."

I CORINTHIANS 13-4

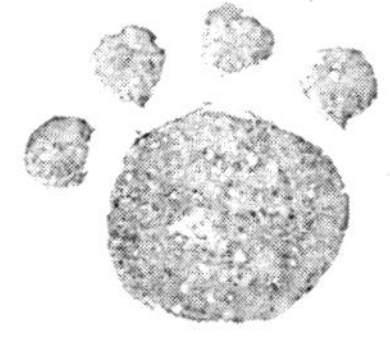

BEAR LEFT